THEY'RE FAMOUSE . . .
THEY'RE FABUMOUSE . . .
AND THEY'RE HERE
TO SAVE THE DAY!
THEY'RE THE

# HEROMICE

AND THESE ARE THEIR
ADVENTURES!

# Geronimo Stilton

# HEROMICE

# TIME MACHINE TROUBLE

Scholastic Inc.

Published by Scholastic Inc., 557 Broadway, New York, NY 10012.



ISBN 978-93-5275-154-9

Text by Geronimo Stilton
Original title *Superger e la supermacchina del tempo*
Original design of the Heromice world by Giuseppe Facciotto and Flavio Ferron
Cover by Giuseppe Facciotto (design) and Daniele Verzini (color)
Illustrations by Luca Usai (pencils), Valeria Cairoli (inks), and Daniele Verzini (color)
Graphics by Francesca Sirianni

Special thanks to Kathryn Cristaldi
Translated by Lidia Tramontozzi
Interior design by Kevin Callahan / BNGO Books

First printing 2018

This edition, August 2024

Printed in India by Saurabh Printers Pvt. Ltd.

When darkness falls over Muskrat City, the Sewer Rats slither into the alleys to cause chaos aboveground. But the citizens of Muskrat City know that there are mysterious figures watching over them, ready to fight evil at all costs.

They are strong, they are invincible, they are fearless — well, almost . . .

They are the Heromice!

# MEET THE HEROMICE!

## GERONIMO SUPERSTILTON

The strongest hero in Muskrat City . . . but he still must learn how to control his powers!

## SWIFTPAWS

Geronimo Superstilton's partner in crimefighting; he can transform his supersuit into anything.

## LADY WONDERWHISKERS

A mysterious mouse with special powers; she always seems to be in the right place at the right time.

## TESS TECHNOPAWS

A cook and scientist who assists the Heromice with every mission.

## ELECTRON AND PROTON

Supersmart mouselets who help the Heromice; they create and operate sophisticated technological gadgets.

# AND THE SEWER RATS!

## TONY SLUDGE

The undisputed leader of the Sewer Rats; known for being tough and mean.

## TERESA SLUDGE

Tony's wife; makes the important decisions for their family.

## ELENA SLUDGE

Tony and Teresa's teenage daughter; has a real weakness for rat metal music.

## SLICKFUR

Sludge's right-hand mouse; the true (and only) brains behind the Sewer Rats.

## ONE, TWO, AND THREE

Bodyguards who act as Sludge's henchmice; they are big, buff, and brainless.

# Frozen Cheese Balls!

It was a frigid Saturday afternoon, but the cold couldn't kill the excitement building in New Mouse City's outdoor stadium. The final soccer game of the season was about to begin. It was a match between the Parmesan City Pawbreakers and the Fabumouse Furbusters.

The bleachers were packed with rodents waving banners, clapping, and shivering from the cold. I was happy I had brought my

Emergency Warm-Up Kit.

Kit included:

1. A superpadded **HAT** with earflaps;
2. A superlong and superthick wool **scarf**;
3. A superhot **thermos** of sweet hot cocoa topped with a double squirt of whipped cream.

Too bad my **Warm-Up Kit** wasn't exactly warming me. In fact, my teeth were **chattering** so hard I was afraid I might need dental work to repair the damage! I'm a newspapermouse, not an arctic explorer!

Oops, how rude. I forgot to introduce myself. My name is Stilton, *Geronimo Stilton*. I'm the publisher of *The Rodent's Gazette*, the most **famouse** newspaper on Mouse Island. I was at the stadium because I was writing an article about the final game of the season.

Time dragged on and on, and the score remained **zero** to **zero**. But at the end of the first half, something happened. The fabumouse Gary Goalmouse, captain of the Pawbreakers, was fouled in the penalty box.

**Tweeeeet!**

The referee blew his whistle and imposed a **penalty kick**.

The Pawbreaker fans were ecstatic. The penalty kick was exactly what they needed to get the advantage point over the Furbusters. With all that **racket**, I could barely hear my cell phone ringing. **FROZEN CHEESE BALLS!** Who was it?

"Boiling cheese blintzes, Geronimo! What's all that noise?" a voice exclaimed.

I knew who it was immediately. It was ***Tess Technopaws***, the kindly cook-scientist at Heromouse Headquarters!

"Good morning, Tess! I'm . . . er . . . at the stadium," I shouted as Gary Goalmouse was about to take the **penalty** kick.

"Sorry to bother you, Geronimo, but Muskrat City desperately needs your—er, I mean Superstilton's—help!"

"But why didn't Swiftpaws call me? Was he kidnapped by the Sewer Rats?"

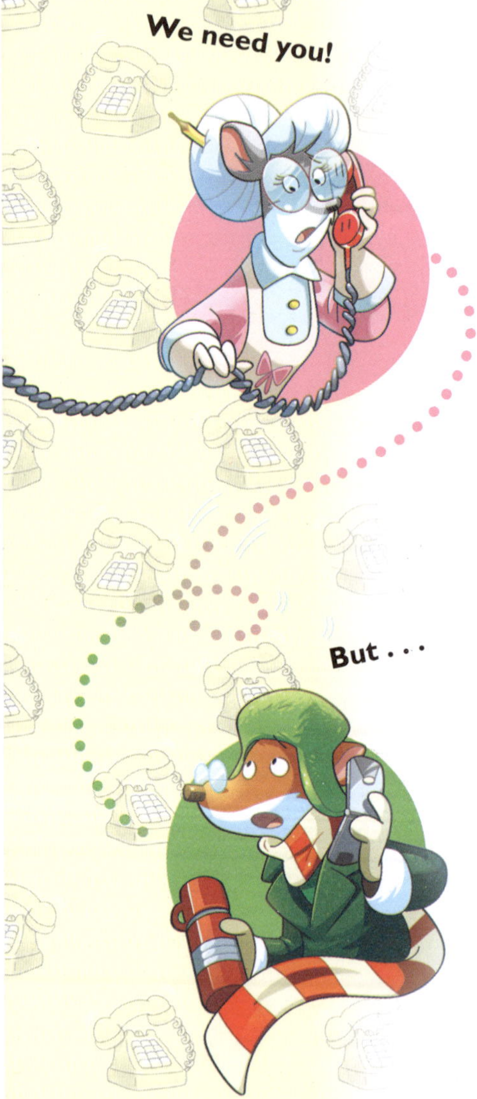


"No!" Tess assured me. "I called because I need all of the HEROMICE!"

"But, um . . . the game, I mean the PAWBREAKERS," I stammered.

"I'll meet you at Heromice Headquarters!" Tess replied firmly before she hung up the phone.

I blinked back TEARS. Poor me! I wouldn't get to see the end of the final game of the season!

Oh, when will

everyone realize that I'm not cut out to be a Heromouse?!

With a sigh, I elbowed my way through the fans to reach the stadium's exit. I hid behind a billboard, took out my SUPERPEN, pressed the secret button, and . . .

ZAP!

A green flash of light enveloped me from the tip of my whiskers to the tip of my tail. In the blink of an eye, I transformed into Superstilton! My paws lifted off the ground, and I shot up into the blue sky at supersonic speed. As I whizzed through the clouds, I watched the stadium grow smaller and smaller and smaller . . .

At that exact moment, Gary Goalmouse took a running start and kicked the ball straight into the net. The last thing I heard before I disappeared into the clouds was

GOOOAL!

# MUSKRAT TOWN?

When I landed at Heromice Headquarters, Swiftpaws was there, twirling around in one of the office chairs.

"Hey, there, **Superpartner**!" he said cheerfully.

"Um, Swiftpaws, do you have any idea why Tess called us?" I asked.

My superpartner stopped twirling. "No clue, Heromouse," he answered, scratching his head. "But I do know one thing: All this spinning is making me SUPERDIZZY!"

Just then, Tess Technopaws arrived. "Welcome, Heromice!" she squeaked. "Thank you for coming."

"No problem," said Swiftpaws. "We Heromice are available 24/7!"

"Well, maybe not 24/7 . . ." I choked, thinking how I would hate to miss another big game. And what about my MOVIE DAY? Or my *library day*? Or my sit-home-and-do-nothing day?

"Follow me," said Tess, leading us to the SECRET BASE.

"I found some very interesting documents concerning a special individual who lived in Muskrat Town over one hundred years ago . . ."

"Muskrat Town?" I repeated.

"Get with the program, Superpartner! That's what Muskrat City was called back in the day!" snorted Swiftpaws.

"That's right," Tess said with a nod. Then she showed us a photo of Muskrat Town.

"Well, hi-ho, little mousey!" Swiftpaws exclaimed. "It looks like a scene from a cowrat movie!"

"The individual I am talking about was a brilliant scientist. His name was Professor

Maximilian Mousemover," Tess continued.

The name sounded so familiar. "Wasn't he the one who was supposed to have traveled through time?" I said.

"That's the one!" Tess confirmed. "There were a lot of stories told about him. In fact, someone said he had invented a TIME MACHINE. But the professor always denied it."

We arrived at the Heromice Secret Base and were greeted by a smiling Proton and ELECTRON.

"Superstilton! Swiftpaws! Look at this!" the pair squeaked with excitement. They are supersmart rodents who help Tess—and the Heromice—on our missions.

We crowded around the control room's supercomputers as Professor Mousemover's picture appeared. He was standing next to a

strange **CONTRAPTION** resembling an old **STAGECOACH**. He was tall with a big, **bushy mustache**.

"I wonder if he ate **SOUP** with that mustache," commented Swiftpaws.

Did I mention my superpartner can be **SUPER-EMBARRASSING** sometimes?

"I don't know about **soup**." Tess chuckled. "But I do know he kept notes. They confirm that the rumors were true. Professor Mousemover really did **build** a time machine!"

"**Timeless cheese sticks!** I don't believe it!" Swiftpaws cried. "Are you sure it's not a joke?"

"The notes and the photos are authentic. We checked everything out," Proton said.

Tess nodded. "The photograph was shot at the **RAT ROCK** quarry more than one hundred years ago! And look at the numbers on the clock at the top of the Time Machine in this photo."

"***Holey cheese!*** That's today's date!" I squeaked in surprise.

If the machine really had traveled through time, it was due to arrive **today**!

TIMER FOR PROGRAMMING TRAVEL THROUGH TIME
DESTINATION
SPECIAL FUEL TANK

At first, we were all so SHOCKED, no one squeaked a word.

Then Electron exclaimed, "If what Tess found is really true, we'll have proof Mousemover is a TIME TRAVELER!"

# A Picnic in Rat Rock

"**Cheesecake!** I still have a hard time believing it!" Swiftpaws exclaimed. "You're not pulling our tails, are you?"

"There's only one way to find out, **Heromice**," Tess replied. "That's why I called you. You can help us find out the truth!"

Immediately, my whiskers started to **tremble** and my fur stood on end.

Don't ask me why, but I had a feeling this latest Heromouse Mission was about to get **superscary**!

"According to Professor Mousemover's

notes," Tess continued, "the *Time Machine* should arrive today at exactly three o'clock."

"But where will it land?" Swiftpaws squeaked, scratching his head.

"That's easy!" Electron said. She pointed to the **monitor**.

A map of Muskrat City popped up on the screen.

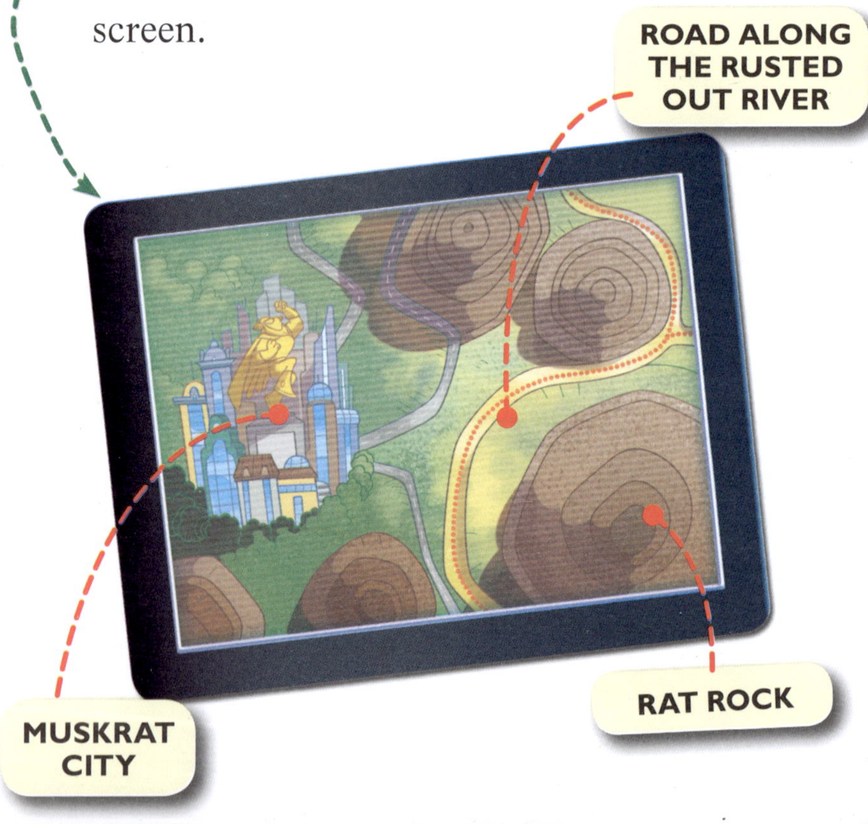

In the photo, the Professor stood in a quarry with a huge mountain behind him. It could only be Rat Rock!

"If Professor Mousemover disappeared at the foot of Rat Rock," Tess concluded, "then there is a pretty good chance that's exactly where he will reappear!"

At that moment, Swiftpaws slapped me on my back so hard my eyes POPPED out of my fur! Well, okay, they didn't really POP out, but you get the picture. It hurt!

"No time to waste, Superpartner!" he squeaked. "We'd better fly there right now at SUPERSONIC SPEED!"

"F-f-fly th-th-th-there?!" I stammered. "Maybe we should go on paw. We could all g-g-go together."

I don't know if you know this, but I am superafraid to fly. It makes me dizzy, nauseous, and downright scared out of my fur! Let's face it, I am just not cut out to be a Heromouse!"

Lucky for me, Tess came to my RESCUE. "Good idea, Superstilton!" she said. "We'll all go to Rat Rock together! And while we're there, we'll have a fabumouse picnic!"

We headed off on paw toward the old abandoned rock quarry. Soon, we were crossing the **Rusted Out River Bridge**.

"Now you know why they call this river **rusted**," said Electron. "It's completely dry!"

"I'll tell you what else is **dry**, my mouth!

It's so hot I'm dying of thirst! And my paws are **KiLLiNG** me! I knew it would've been easier if we flew!" Swiftpaws said. "Why don't we . . ."

My superpartner **whined** on and on until at last we reached the quarry.

"Now we can find out if Professor Mousemover's invention really works!" squeaked Tess excitedly.

I looked at the clock. In **two minutes**, Professor Mousemover would be arriving from the past. In fact, right at that exact moment, we heard a noise . . .

**KZOOOOm!**

A strange apparatus **ZOOMED** toward us from the depths of the quarry! We barely had time to hit the ground before the mysterious machine raced past us and finished its journey in a cloud of dust, *smoke*, and ELECTRICAL SPARKS.

SCREECH!

BONK!

ZAAAAP!

Blistering blue cheese! It really was Professor Mousemover's **TIME MACHINE**!

Blistering blue cheese!
Help!

Yippeeeee!

# It Worked!

The tires of the Time Machine screeched to a halt with a metallic sound. A distinguished, dusty rodent jumped up from the driver's seat.

"Good ol' Gouda!" he exclaimed. "It worked!"

"I — I don't believe it!" Electron gasped. "Tess was right!"

It was the rodent we had seen on the computer screen at Heromice Headquarters! Professor Mousemover looked just like his picture. He was dressed like an old-fashioned train conductor and sported a thick, bushy mustache.

"Please excuse my ignorance," he said with a friendly voice. "Could you tell me what year this is?"

Good morning!
Ooooh . . .
Gulp!
The Time Machine . . .

We stared at him, our snouts hanging open in shock.

"Extraordinary . . ." was the only thing Tess could squeak.

Professor Mousemover smiled.

"Pardon my bad manners, madam," he said, taking her paw in his. "Such an ENCHANTING rodent deserves a proper greeting." He kissed her paw lightly.

"Oh!" squeaked a flattered Tess.

When we got over our surprise, we bombarded the professor with a million questions.

"Where do you come from?"

"When did you leave?"

"What was the weather like in **Muskrat Town**?"

He confirmed all our theories. He had left from **Rat Rock** more than one hundred years ago and reappeared over one **one hundred** years later! If I hadn't seen it with my own eyes, I would have thought someone was pulling my paw!

"And now, may I give you all a guided tour of my Time Machine?" the professor asked.

"Yes!" shouted Electron and Proton, jumping **UP** and **DOWN**. I wanted to jump, too, but I forced myself just to nod enthusiastically.

After the professor finished showing us the machine, Tess grew **serious**.

"Dear Professor Mousemover, yours is an extraordinary invention. I'm sure you'll use it wisely. I can't imagine what would happen if it fell into the **wrong** paws . . ."

"Oh, don't worry, madam," Professor Mousemover assured her. "This was just a **TEST DRIVE**. I don't think I'll ever use my machine again. I just wanted to

see if my calculations were correct. And, to be perfectly honest with you, I wanted to take a peek at the future. Once I go back to Muskrat Town, I'll dismantle the machine piece by piece. And I'll destroy all my notes."

"You're very wise," said Tess, smiling.

"It's my duty, dear colleague," answered the professor. "Traveling through time could be very dangerous. I don't want to run the risk of having my invention end up in the paws of evil and selfish rodents."

Suddenly, the professor's snout grew pale. He was staring at a red blinking light on the Time Machine's control panel.

"Oh no," he sputtered, looking worried.

I glanced down and noticed a dial underneath the blinking light. A tiny needle pointed to the word "empty". Something told me the professor was about to tell us some bad news.

"The Time Machine runs on Swiss cheese, and the tank is **empty**! If I can't get it filled, I'll never be able to return to the p-p-present, I mean, the p-p-past, I mean . . ." the professor stuttered.

"That shouldn't be a problem," Tess replied. "After all, we have Swiss cheese in the present . . . um, I mean, your future!" Tess blushed.

"Yes, don't worry, Professor!" Swiftpaws exclaimed

confidently. "Superstilton will be superhappy to assist you! Won't you, Superpartner?"

"Well . . . actually . . . I . . ." I muttered.

Swiftpaws ignored my protests.

"Don't be shy, Superstilton. With your superpowers, you can whip up tons of Swiss cheese for the professor!"

# A Tankful of Swiss Cheese

Everyone stared at me expectantly. They were waiting for me to **ACTIVATE** my superpowers. But there was one small problem. I wasn't exactly sure how my ***SUPERPOWERS*** worked!

How many times did I have to say it — I'm not cut out to be a Heromouse!

Before I could protest again, Swiftpaws elbowed me in the side. "Well, what are you waiting for, Superstilton? I'm sure the professor doesn't have all day. Where's that **Swiss**?"

"Oh, **showers of mozzarella**!" I snorted in frustration. "I don't know how."

But before I could say another word, a

shower of **mozzarella balls** rained down from the sky.

I had **ACCIDENTALLY** activated my cheesy superpowers!

"**Impressive!**" exclaimed Professor Mousemover, staring at the cheese balls

now bouncing on the ground.

"Ahem . . . Superstilton," said Electron clearing her throat. "We don't need mozzarella, we need Swiss."

"Concentrate, Heromouse!" squeaked Swiftpaws. "Try again!"

Exasperated, I yelled, "Super Swiss cheese! I can't do it!"

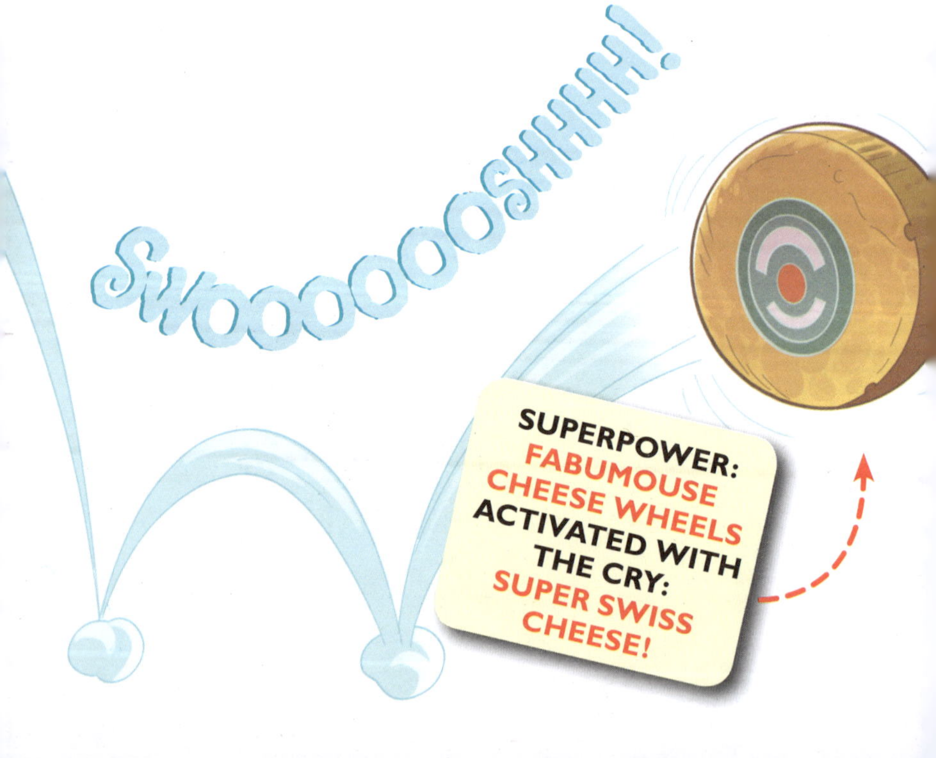

Suddenly, a delicious-smelling wheel of Swiss cheese came **rolling** toward us at full speed!

"**REMARKABLE!**" cried Professor Mousemover. "Rodents of the future can do the most exceptional things!"

Using the camping stove Proton brought, we **melted** the cheese

and began filling the Time Machine's tank.

The Time Machine immediately started to CHUG.

"Thank you," Professor Mousemover said with a smile. "Now I'll have enough FUEL to go home."

As the machine was filling, Proton suggested we take the professor for a quick tour of Muskrat City.

"That would be fabumouse," the Professor agreed.

"We just need someone to stay behind to keep an eye on the machine. We can never be too CAUTIOUS," Tess warned.

"Superstilton and I can do it," my superpartner volunteered, wiggling his eyebrows and winking at me. Uh-oh. Whenever Swiftpaws gets that look on his snout, I know he's about to propose some crazy stunt. What was it this time?

It didn't take long to find out. As soon as everyone had left, Swiftpaws pointed to the **mozzarella balls** that had rained down on us earlier.

"Someone needs to make this cheese *disappear*, right, Superpartner?" He chuckled.

Soon, Swiftpaws and I were gorging ourselves on **SUPER-SIZED** cheese balls.

Of course, eating all of that cheese made us supersleepy.

"I could go for a nap," Swiftpaws said with a **YAWN**.

Two minutes later, we were both **snoring** away like my great uncle Handyrat's eardrum-piercing electric chain saw!

ZZZZZZZZZZZZZZZZ!

I woke up when Swiftpaws **ELBOWED** me in the side.

VRRRRRR

"Hey, Superstilton! Quit snoring!" he growled. "You're so **LOUD**. I can't even hear my own dreams!"

I opened one eye.

"I wasn't *snoring*," I mumbled.

"Well, if it's not you, then what's all that noise?"

"N-noise?" I said.

My eyes popped open in alarm.

Rotten cheese rinds! I heard it, too!

**VRRRRRR . . .**

It was a sort of a buzz . . .

**VRRRRRR . . .**

It became louder and louder!

**VRRRRRR . . .**

A second later, the Sewer Rats' **Drillmobile** came blasting out of the quarry's depths. Nooooooo!

But it's . . .
the Drillmobile!

# PLOP! PLOP! PLOP!

Tony Sludge was the first to climb out of the strange-looking car.

"There it is!" he squeaked happily. "The famouse **Time Machine**!"

Swiftpaws and I looked at each other, surprised. How did the **SEWER RATS** know about the professor's machine?

Just then Tony spotted us. "Well, well," he snarled. "If it isn't the *Superpests*! Take care of them, boys! I don't need any troublemakers today!"

With that, **ONE**, **TWO**, and **THREE**, Sludge's massive bodyguards, piled out of the Drillmobile.

Sludge's right-hand mouse, **SLICKFUR**, was right behind them. He pointed an odd horn at us and yelled, “Stop where you are, Superfools!”

“You don’t scare us, Cheeseface!” snorted Swiftpaws.

Suddenly, Slickfur activated the weird device and . . . **Plop! Plop! Plop!**

A volley of gigantic soap bubbles *streamed* out.

**PLOP! PLOP! PLOP!**

Suddenly, one of the massive bubbles **swallowed** me whole!

"What happened?" exclaimed Swiftpaws. He was **TRAPPED** inside another bubble.

"H-how do we g-g-get out of here?" I stammered.

"Forget it, Superpests!" Slickfur snorted. "**You can't!**"

Swiftpaws and I tried pulling, **PINCHING**, and gnawing our way out, but the bubbles wouldn't break.

"My superbubbles are unpoppable!" cackled Slickfur. "You'll never escape!"

Still, Swiftpaws and I kept trying. My superpartner even tried using his superpowers to turn himself into a pair of SUPERSCISSORS. But nothing worked!

"That'll teach you not to MEDDLE!" Tony laughed. "And now, Mousemover's invention will be mine! All mine!"

"Don't you mean ours?!" said a third rat. He had just emerged from the Drillmobile.

"Boiling cheese blintzes!" cried Swiftpaws. "Who is that?"

Gulp! My fur stood on end.

The rat stepping out of the Drillmobile looked exactly like Tony Sludge, except for his clothes. Instead of a three-piece suit, he wore a cowrat hat, a red bandanna around his neck, and cowrat boots.

"Let me introduce myself, Superclowns," snickered the new arrival. "My name is . . ."

"Butch Sludge!" exclaimed Tony Sludge, interrupting him. "The most wanted criminal in Muskrat Town—and my great-great-grandfather!"

What?!?
Gulp!
Say hello to Butch Sludge!
Har, har, har!

# THE TERROR OF MUSKRAT TOWN!

"Did you say great-great-grandfather?!" asked Swiftpaws.

"**Pests of the present**, you're facing the Terror of Muskrat Town!" Butch said, introducing himself. "This morning, I hid inside Mousemover's Time Machine. Then, while you two clowns were **Snoozing**, I called my great-great-grandson here."

My heart **dropped**. What could the great-great-grandfather of the **rotten** Tony Sludge be up to? Something told me he hadn't arrived for a friendly family reunion!

"Thanks to my great-great-grandson, I now have some **evil** gadgets to take back with me to the past. Then I will take over

Muskrat Town once and for all!"

We watched helplessly as Tony's henchmice loaded the Time Machine with Slickfur's DEADLY inventions:

1. UNPOPPABLE BUBBLE SQUIRTER
2. TANKS OF LOUD LAUGHTER
3. Mechanical fleas

"Watch and weep, SUPERDUDS! Your days are numbered!" boasted Tony. "As soon as the Time Machine is loaded, my great-great-grandfather will—"

"Let me talk, Grandson!" Butch Sludge interrupted him. "I'll go back to the past, take over Muskrat Town and—"

"The future will be changed!" Tony finished. "Tomorrow we'll all wake up in a world where Sewer Rats reign over Muskrat City!"

At that moment, the Time Machine beeped loudly. DING, DING, DING!

Twisted cattails! The machine was filled and ready to go!

How could we stop

Butch from leaving when we were stuck in **UNPOPPABLE** bubbles?!

Lucky for us, Tess and the professor arrived back at the quarry just at that moment.

"Butch Sludge?! What are you doing here?" Professor Mousemover cried in disbelief.

Butch let out a low, evil laugh. "Surprise!" shrieked the time-traveling criminal. "My great-great-grandson and I have a mission to complete!"

Tess and the professor exchanged terrified looks. For a moment, they were squeakless. Finally, Tess found her voice. "Beware, Sewer Rats!" she warned. "Changing history could have terrible consequences!"

Butch burst out laughing. "You mean like us Sewer Rats taking over the whole city?!"

"Heh, heh, heh, that's the plan!" snickered Tony.

I was about to break out in sobs when a vision appeared before my eyes. A female mouse with LONG, *silky* blonde hair stood there looking down at the rock quarry.

***Great Gouda!*** It was the smart, *strong*, and courageous Lady Wonderwhiskers!

# A Battle to the Last Bubble

With an *acrobatic* leap, the super-rodent of my dreams was by our side.

"Get your paws off the Time Machine, Sewer Slime!" she exclaimed.

Ahhhhhh! Lady Wonderwhiskers. What **STRENGTH**, what **agility**, what unmistakable **grace**!

"What are you waiting for?" Tony roared to his henchmice. "Get her!"

One, Two, and Three sprang into action.

**POW!**

**WHAM!**

**KAPOW!**

But with a couple of **swift** karate moves, Lady Wonderwhiskers knocked them down! Massaging their **lumps**, the Rats slowly climbed back to their paws. Swiftpaws and I were still powerless prisoners in our **SUPERBUBBLES**.

"They're getting up!" I squeaked. "**Watch out**, Lady Wonderwhiskers!"

I know, Lady Wonderwhiskers is **tough**, but she was totally outnumbered!

I gnashed my teeth in frustration.

"Psssst, Superstilton! I've got an idea," Swiftpaws whispered. Then he shouted at the top of his lungs,

**"Activate Super Mega-Fork Mode!"**

**ZAAP!**

Swiftpaws used his superpowers to change into a **gigantic** yellow fork. Then he tried to pierce the bubble.

**Boiiing!**

The tip of the fork bounced back. It hadn't even scratched the surface of the transparent bubble!

Rotten cheese rinds! Those bubbles were stronger than my cousin Musclemouse!

All of a sudden, we heard a voice.

"I'll save you, Heromice!"

It was Proton.

"You'll save us?" Swiftpaws replied. "But we're the HEROMICE! If we can't break the —"

Before he could finish, Proton poured a *stream* of clear liquid onto the giant bubbles.

**Pop! Pop!**

The bubbles vanished instantly.

"Super Swiss slices!" Swiftpaws shouted. "What did you use? A superpower fluid? A rat repellent liquid? Antibubble drops?"

"It's just water, Swiftpaws!" laughed Proton. "The Sewer Rats' soap may be ultra-

resistant, but it's still soap. Contact with WATER dissolves it!"

"Good work, Proton!" I chuckled.

"Stop FLAPPING your jaws, Superstilton!" exclaimed Swiftpaws. He yanked me back to my duties. "Lady Wonderwhiskers is in trouble!"

One, Two, and Three had surrounded our superfriend. Slickfur was pointing his lethal bubble-shooter at her. **Holey cheddar sticks!** I was scared out of my fur, but I had to do something! We had to help her!

# Destination: Muskrat Town!

Swiftpaws and I scampered over to Lady Wonderwhiskers, but she waved us off.

"Go get Butch, Heromice!" she exclaimed. "He's about to board the Time Machine!"

Slimy cheese balls!

Lady Wonderwhiskers was right! There wasn't a second to lose. Butch Sludge was frantically punching buttons and flipping levers on the control panel of the Time Machine.

"Muskrat Town, here I come!" he jeered. "Heh, heh, heh!"

"Holey hot mozzarella melt!" exclaimed Professor Mousemover. "You have to stop him from getting away!"

With a **leap**, I threw myself at Tony Sludge's great-great-grandfather. Meanwhile, Swiftpaws jumped into the TIME MACHINE.

Lady Wonderwhiskers shook off One, Two, and Three and grabbed on to the side of the machine. I grabbed the other side.

Swiftpaws let out his battle cry:

**"HEROMICE IN ACTION!"**

ZZZZZOOO

The Time Machine took off with a jolt. We were moving at SUPERSONIC speed.

"Hang on!" Swiftpaws yelled.

We CLUNG with all our might as the machine sped away like a rocket.

"Rat-munching rattlesnakes!" squeaked Swiftpaws. "We're traveling through time!"

Zzzap!

Zzzap!

Zzzap!

om!
Aaaaaahhh!
Heeeeelp!
Squeak!

A discharge of electrical shocks **zapped** around us. Suddenly, we were inside a mega-vortex that traveled through time and space, connecting the present to the past.

I got **zapped** right on my tail!

"Yeowwww!" I shrieked. I was so scared, I *slipped* and let go of my grip. But just when I thought I was a goner who was going to be **lost in time**, Lady Wonderwhiskers grabbed my paw!

She looked at me with her kind, ***sparkling blue eyes*** and squeaked, "I've got you, Superstilton!"

My heart swelled. What courage! What skill! What a mouse!

"I see something ahead!" Swiftpaws yelled, **interrupting** my thoughts. "I think we've arrived at our destination!"

**Flying cheese balls!** What a fabumouse trip!

# WELCOME TO THE PAST

The **TIME MACHINE** stopped. We were in the exact place where it had taken off, in the **ROCK** quarry.

Lady Wonderwhiskers let go of my paw, and I fell like a fifty-pound block of cheddar!

Oh, how **embarrassing**!

"Everything okay, Superstilton?" the heromouse of my dreams asked.

"Um, yes, thank me, I mean, thank you, er, not me . . ."

I stammered. Oh, why do I always act like a *superfool* when I'm around the **amazing** Lady Wonderwhiskers?!

"Snap out of it, Superstilton!" Swiftpaws interrupted. "Butch Sludge is getting away!"

I spotted Tony's great-great-grandfather **SLINKING** away into the past. He was gripping an unpoppable bubble squirter in his **DIRTY** little paws.

"Hold it right there, Butch Sludge!" I shouted. "You're not going to use the inventions of the **future** to make a mess of the **past**!"

"Oh, yeah?" he snickered. "Who's gonna stop me?!"

"We are!" Swiftpaws squeaked.

"Are you sure, **SUPERMEDDLERS**?"

That's when we heard a noise behind us. Four Sewer Rats from the **wild west** scampered toward us from behind some rocks. The first was a **skinny** rat dressed in black. Except for the **MUSTACHE**, he looked almost identical to Slickfur.

"Say hello to **CHEESITO**, my right-hand rat." Butch snickered.

Then he pointed to three **muscular** rats wearing sombreros. They looked identical to One, Two, and Three!

"And these are **ONE**, **TWO**, and **THREE**, my bodyguards!"

The thugs glared at us with **beady** eyes.

Rats! I was so, so

scared I almost fainted.

But not Swiftpaws.

"**Sewer Rats**

of the past,"

he shouted

calmly.

"Prepare to

face off with the

**Heromice** of the future!"

But just then we heard a GURGLING sound.

PLOP!

PLOP!

PLOP!

**Watery cheese dip!**

Butch had once again captured us in prisonlike superbubbles!

This time, Swiftpaws and I were trapped inside one **MASSIVE** bubble.

"**Double trouble bubble!**" exclaimed Swiftpaws. "Not again!"

Meanwhile, Lady Wonderwhiskers stared helplessly at us from inside her own **UNPOPPABLE** superbubble.

"How do we get out of these things?" she groaned.

"Boss, who are these **party-poopers**?" asked Cheesito, looking at us as if we were lab rats.

"Just three **SUPERMEDDLERS** from the future. Don't worry. They won't give us any more trouble." Butch snickered.

Uno, Dos, and Tres gathered around their leader.

"Now that the **SUPERPESTS** are out of the way, we can take a **cheese break**," said the henchmice.

But Butch flew into a rage.

"I'm the boss!" he squeaked. "I say what we do! Now quit **yapping** and unload all of the inventions from the **future** from the Time Machine. We've got a town to take over!"

When the henchmice finished **unloading** the Time Machine, they turned to Butch. "What next, Boss?" they asked.

"Follow me, mice!" Butch commanded. "It's time we pay a visit to the **bank**. We'll need lots of **money** if we're going to take over Muskrat Town! **HEH, HEH, HEH!**"

We watched in horror as Butch and the rest of the sewer rats headed for Muskrat Town, armed with Slickfur's **inventions**.

"We've got to stop them!" I wailed. If only I knew how.

# Rolling Toward Rusted Out River

"Superstilton's right!" Lady Wonderwhiskers squeaked as we watched the departing BANDITOS. "We can't just stand here twiddling our paws!"

"Okay, then," replied Swiftpaws. "Have any ideas on how to get out of these superbubbles, Lady Wonderwhiskers?"

Lady Wonderwhiskers shook her head.

"If we only had some WATER," I moaned. Then I started thinking. "Hmm . . . there is one river in this area, RUSTED OUT RIVER. But it's been dry for a long time."

"That's it!" Lady Wonderwhiskers cried.

"You're a supergenius, Superstilton!"

I had no idea what the heromouse of my dreams was talking about, but who was I to argue?

"Right now we're in the PAST. And in the past, RUSTED OUT RIVER was probably a real river!" Lady Wonderwhiskers explained. "If we can find the river, we can dissolve these bubbles!"

"Great idea!" Swiftpaws shouted.

"But how can we move when we're stuck in these superbubbles?" I asked.

"That's simple," Lady Wonderwhiskers replied. "We roll them!"

My whiskers began to tremble. But how could I say no? The safety of both Muskrat Town and Muskrat City was at stake!

And so we began to roll. Somehow,

Lady Wonderwhiskers seemed to roll along with a natural ease and grace. Swiftpaws and I were the exact opposite.

"Superstilton, be careful! You're **stepping** on my cape!"

"Well, you're on my tail!"

We screamed at each other as the bubble rolled ***FASTER*** and ***FASTER***. Soon, we were bouncing along, completely out of control.

Boing,
boing,
boing!

Luckily, we landed in the river. The bubble burst with a giant **pop**!

Swiftpaws and I looked like **drowned** rats, but we were free.

"Good job, Lady Wonderwhiskers! Your plan worked!" I said.

The heromouse grinned proudly. "Thanks, Superstilton," she squeaked. Then she grew serious. "But how can we beat **Butch** and his **henchmice** to the bank?!"

Swiftpaws held up a paw. "I've got this, heropartners!" he announced. Then he cleared his throat.

"Activate **SUPERSIDECAR MODE**!" he yelled.

**VROOM!**

**VROOOM!**

**VROOOOM!**

Using his superpowers, Swiftpaws had transformed himself into a yellow motorcycle with a sidecar!

I gulped. Did I mention I'm afraid of motorcycles? And sidecars?

"M-m-m-maybe we should walk instead," I stammered.

"Don't be afraid, Superstilton," said Lady Wonderwhiskers encouragingly as she got into the driver's seat. "You can do it!"

I CHEWED my whiskers.

"Oh, SUPERSONIC space cheese!" Swiftpaws yelped. "Move it, Superstilton!"

So I took a DEEP breath and climbed on board.

Lady Wonderwhiskers hit the gas, and the engine ROARED to life.

VRRRRO

We took off in a FLASH, kicking up a cloud of dust behind us. Destination: Muskrat Town!

OOM!
Here we go!
Heeeeelp!
USKRAT
TOWN

# THE GREAT BANK ROBBERY

When we got to town, we were amazed. We felt like we were in a WESTERN movie! As we scurried through the main street, several rodents shot us looks of fear.

It was clear that the townsmice weren't used to seeing rodents with CAPES and supercostumes in roaring YELLOW MOTORCYCLES WITH SIDECARS!

"Let me see if I can WARM up the crowd," suggested Swiftpaws.

I tried to stop him. I had a feeling *squeaking* would just make things worse. But Swiftpaws approached a group of rodents anyway.

"Excuse us, dear ancestors," he began.

"Would you mind telling us where the **bank** is? We come from the future, and we have to stop a bank robbery . . ."

They ran away as fast as their little **paws** could carry them!

As the rodents ran, we heard **noises** coming from the other end of the street.

"**That way!**" cried Lady Wonderwhiskers.

We ran toward the noise. It was coming from the **Muskrat Bank**! Then we saw flashes of light and soap bubbles coming out of the windows and door.

BUTCH and his henchmice were using the devices that Slickfur had developed for the heist of the century!

Meanwhile, a small group of rodents watched cautiously from behind a **wagon**.

Then one of them came toward us. **Smoky mozzarella!** That rodent looked exactly like Commissioner Ratford! The only difference was that he was wearing a **cowrat hat** and had a **GOLD STAR** pinned to his vest.

"I'm Sheriff Ratford," he said, introducing himself. "Who are you?"

"Well, um, we are, you see, er . . ." I mumbled.

Cheese niblets! How could I tell Sheriff Ratford we were **Heromice** who had come from the future?! Luckily, right then a loud rumble erupted from inside the bank.

"Sorry to run," Lady Wonderwhiskers squeaked. "We have to stop Butch Sludge and his henchmice before it's too late!"

"Yes, of course, but please be careful," Sheriff Ratford warned us. "The Sewer Rats are using some pretty strange-looking CONTRAPTIONS."

Swiftpaws puffed up his fur. "We'll take care of it Commiss—er, I mean, Sheriff!" he exclaimed.

And that's when a laser beam zapped past

me and Singed my whiskers!

"***Sizzling Swiss bits!*** Are you sure we n-n-need to go in there right n-n-now?" I stammered. "I'm not sure if I told you, but I'm too fond of my fur!"

"Oh, stop that whining, Superstilton!" Swiftpaws shouted as he dashed past me and headed straight for the bank.

"HEROMICE IN ACTION!"

he cried.

# You Again?

My paws were **shaking** as I followed Swiftpaws and Lady Wonderwhiskers into the bank. Super Swiss slices! Those rotten Sewer Rats had tied up the bank manager like a supersausage!

Cheesito, Uno, Dos, and Tres were pointing the bubble squirters at the bank tellers.

"I don't see **Butch Sludge** anywhere!" cried Swiftpaws.

"Over there!" Lady Wonderwhiskers shrieked, pointing to the office.

Tony's great-great-grandfather was in a corner, **HUNCHED** over by the manager's desk. He had *blown* up the safe and was filling a huge **sack** with money. As we approached, he whirled around.

Stop, thieves!
You again!?
Gulp!

"**Impossible!**" he groaned. "You three again?!"

"That's right!" Lady Wonderwhiskers exclaimed. Then she leapt through the air, hurtling herself toward him. "Nothing is **impossible** for us Heromice!"

It looked like it was all over for Butch until the evil Cheesito raced into the room. He pointed his bubble squirter and pulled the trigger . . .

**PLOP! PLOP! PLOP!**

But Swiftpaws was faster.

"*Activate Hair Dryer Mode!*" he squeaked just in time. In a **flash**, his cape changed into a huge hair dryer. He aimed it at Cheesito.

**Whoosh!**

The superbubble of indestructible soap blew back toward Cheesito, covering him completely. The slimy rat was trapped like a lab specimen!

Butch turned to his henchmice, **ONE**, **TWO**, and **THREE**. "Well, what are you waiting for, you fools?" he squeaked. "Get them!"

The three criminals went after Lady Wonderwhiskers.

But they were no match for her. "Give it up, **SEWER SLIME**!" the Heromouse cried.

She twirled an enormouse lasso over her head with expert style and ease. Then she threw it at Butch Sludge's henchmice, tying them up **tight**.

Uno, Dos, and Tres fell like dominos on top of each other.

BOINK! BOINK! BOINK!

The only one left standing was Butch. The dangerous gang leader was hightailing it for the rear exit.

"Butch is getting away with the loot!" cried Lady Wonderwhiskers.

"**Chunky cheese wheels!**" I shouted. "Not this time!"

At those words, my cheesy superpowers activated.

RUMMMMMMBLE!

SUPERPOWER:
AN AVALANCHE OF CHEESE WHEELS
ACTIVATED WITH THE CRY:
"CHUNKY CHEESE WHEELS!"
Nice try, Sewer Slime!
Wow!

Incredible!
Grrrrrr . . .
Hee, hee, hee!

An avalanche of cheese wheels **rained** down on Butch, blocking his getaway.

"**GET ME OUT OF HERE!**" Butch shouted from beneath the mound of cheese.

At that moment, Sheriff Ratford marched through the front door. He looked around in **shock**.

"Well, I'll be darned!" he exclaimed. "You mice sure have an interesting way of catching the crooks!"

While Ratford and his deputies rounded up Butch and his gang, Lady Wonderwhiskers collected all of Cheesito's gadgets.

"Let's get these back to the **future**, Heromice," she said. "No one should mess around with the course of time!"

Sheriff Ratford strode over and shook each of our paws.

"I don't know **WHO** you are or *where*

you come from, but you are our heroes," he said. "You'll always be welcome in Muskrat Town!"

"Thanks, Sheriff," I said, smiling. "We love Muskrat City, er, I mean, Muskrat Town. Not that we've ever been here. I mean, not really. Er . . ."

"Ahem, Heromice," interrupted Lady Wonderwhiskers. "I think it's time we return home."

# Back . . . to the Present

We hopped into the Time Machine and zoomed back to the present day. Lady Wonderwhiskers had cleverly programmed the machine so that we would reappear ten minutes after we had left. When we arrived, Tess, Electron, Proton, and Professor Mousemover were waiting for us in RAT ROCK quarry.

"Welcome back!" they squeaked. "What happened? Did you take care of Butch?"

"I think it's safe to say that Butch and his

gang won't be time traveling again for a **long**, **long** time!" Lady Wonderwhiskers announced with a grin.

Suddenly, I remembered something.

"Wait, what happened to Tony Sludge?" I asked.

Tess smiled.

"Tony and his henchrats went back to the sewers in the **Drillmobile** as soon as you left. The Sewer Rats were convinced they had changed HISTORY and were now in control of Muskrat City." She chuckled.

"Those sewer slugs underestimated the Heromice once again!" Swiftpaws shouted triumphantly.

Professor Mousemover cleared his throat. "But how can you be so sure your trip to **Muskrat Town** didn't change things?" he asked, scratching his head.

Proton pulled open his laptop and began CLICKING away. He showed the professor how he had connected his computer to Muskrat City's surveillance cameras. Then he explained how he was able to use the cameras to see what was going on in Muskrat City.

Poor Professor Mousemover looked completely **bewildered**. I wasn't surprised. The professor had never even seen a **COMPUTER** before!

Proton continued **clicking** away at his keyboard. "I was also able to set up a camera so that we can see what's going on down in the sewers of **Rottington**," he explained. "Let's take a look."

Everyone stared at the monitor. At first everything looked calm in Rottington.

But then the image changed. We were

looking at Tony's living room on the screen. The leader of the Sewer Rats **paced** back and forth like a crazed rat.

"Tony, **Sweetpaws**, try to calm down," his wife, Teresa, soothed him.

But Tony Sludge looked like he was about to explode with **anger**!

"Blocked up sewer pipes! What went wrong? By this time Butch should have taken over Muskrat Town. He should have changed history! By now, I should be the ruler, the chief, the head Rato of Muskrat City! Oh, where did I go wrong? Where? Where? Where?" he sobbed.

"It looks like old Sewer Sludge is down in the dumps *and* the sewer." Swiftpaws chuckled.

Everyone **burst** out laughing.

# Good-bye, Professor Mousemover!

It was time for Professor Mousemover to return home. But before he could leave, we had to refill the fuel tank of the *Time Machine* with Swiss cheese. How did I **activate** my superpowers again? Was it "Holey Swiss cheese" or "Cheesy Swiss chunks"?

"Come on, Superstilton!" Swiftpaws scolded me. "We don't have all day!"

"**SUPER SWISS CHEESE!** I'm trying!" I wailed.

At those words, my cheesy superpowers kicked in.

When the tank was full, Mousemover climbed aboard the Time Machine.

"Farewell, friends! The future is very interesting, but I think it's a little too **chaotic** for an old-fashioned rodent like me," he said apologetically. "Loud picture screens, gigantic bubbles that are impossible to pop, machines that come out of the ground, showers of cheese . . . the past is just so much **QUIETER**."

I thought about what the professor had said. It was hard to imagine a world without our TVs and **cell phones**, but maybe a little quiet wasn't really so bad. I started to think about my next vacation. Maybe I could go to a **quiet** island with a **quiet** beach in the middle of a **quiet**, out-of-the-way ocean. I could leave all my ***gadgets*** at home and just bring a few good books.

"Thank you for everything, Heromice!" the professor said, interrupting my daydream.

He assured Tess he'd take apart the **Time Machine** as soon as he got home. Then the professor waved good-bye and the Time Machine took off in a burst of **electrical sparks**. Unfortunately, one of them **ZAPPED** Swiftpaws in the paw.

"Ouch!" he cried.

"I think it's **time** I go, too," I said, checking my watch.

"Not so fast, Superstilton!" Swiftpaws exclaimed, nursing his injury. "Don't you have **time** for a little bite to eat?"

Dear rodent friends, how could I refuse? I was **starving**! In fact, I felt as if I hadn't eaten in a **century**!

We headed back to ***HEROMICE HEADQUARTERS***. Tess set the table. Then

Good-bye, my frieeeeends . . .
So long!
Have a good trip!
Ouch!

she brought out a platter of delicious-looking sandwiches and a pitcher of ice-cold cheese milkshakes.

I was so hungry I was practically drooling on my plate. Oh, how embarrassing!

# BACK TO SQUARE ONE!

After I stuffed myself with Tess's super-duper sandwiches, I said good-bye to my friends and soared off into the sky, heading straight toward New Mouse City.

Suddenly, I remembered the match between the Parmesan City Pawbreakers and the Fabumouse Furbusters! I wondered how the game had ended.

I flew over the stadium and saw that the bleachers were still packed with fans. The teams were entering the field at that very moment!

**Huh?! How could that be possible?** The game had taken place the day before.

I was **SUPERSURE** of this! Cheesewhiskers! I had to find out what had happened.

I landed in the parking lot and rushed up to the gate.

"Excuse me. Didn't this game end **yesterday**?" I asked the ticket agent.

He looked at me as if I had *five* heads and *three* tails.

"Did you just come from another planet?" He laughed.

"Actually, I, well, um . . . It's a **long** story," I babbled.

"So you don't know what **happened**?" the mouse asked, still in shock.

"Uh, no," I mumbled. How could I explain that I had been in another time zone . . . a time zone from the **PAST**!

"Well, yesterday at the end of the first half, a huge storm broke out,"

he explained. "The field got soaked, and the players couldn't see their own whiskers in front of their snouts!"

Apparently, the managers decided to call off the game. It had been rescheduled for today! What luck! I would still be able to SEE the match and write my article for the newspaper!

And if there is one thing I had learned that week, it's this: Nothing is impossible when time is on your side. And nothing is IMPOSSIBLE for the Heromice!

# Be sure to read all my fabumouse adventures!

#1 Lost Treasure of the Emerald Eye

#2 The Curse of the Cheese Pyramid

#3 Cat and Mouse in a Haunted House

#4 I'm Too Fond of My Fur!

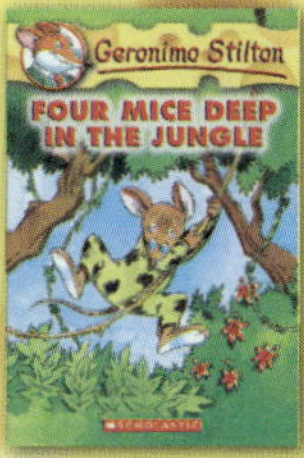


#5 Four Mice Deep in the Jungle

#6 Paws Off, Cheddarface!

#7 Red Pizzas for a Blue Count

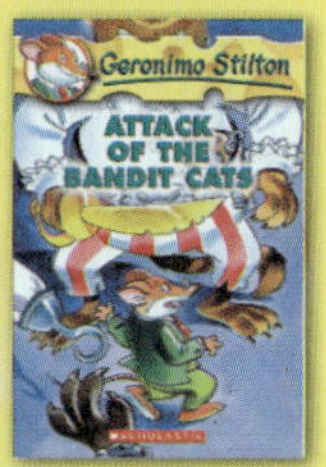


#8 Attack of the Bandit Cats

#9 A Fabumouse Vacation for Geronimo

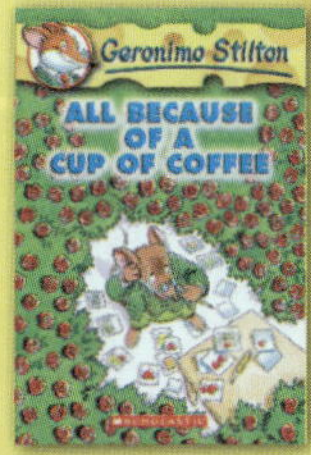


#10 All Because of a Cup of Coffee

#11 It's Halloween, You 'Fraidy Mouse!

#12 Merry Christmas, Geronimo!

#13 The Phantom of the Subway

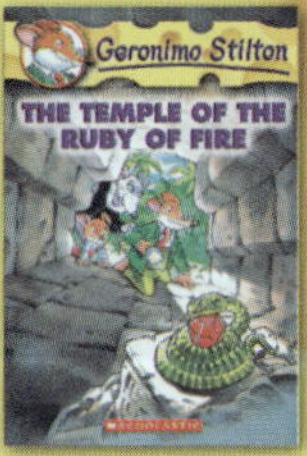


#14 The Temple of the Ruby of Fire

#15 The Mona Mousa Code

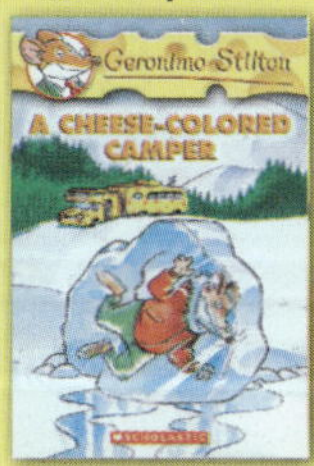


#16 A Cheese-Colored Camper

#17 Watch Your Whiskers, Stilton!

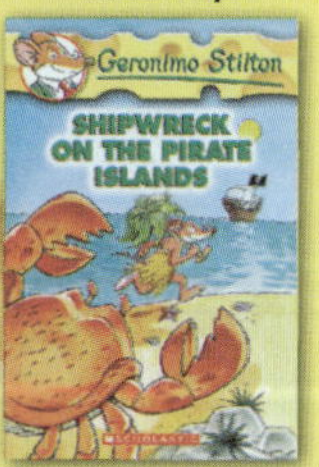


#18 Shipwreck on the Pirate Islands

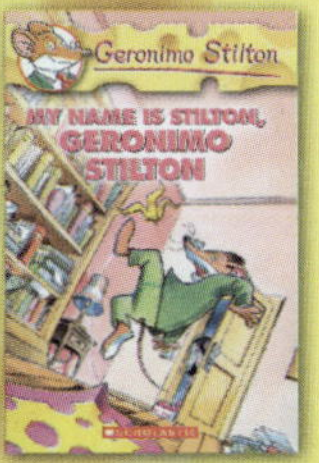


#19 My Name Is Stilton, Geronimo Stilton

#20 Surf's Up, Geronimo!

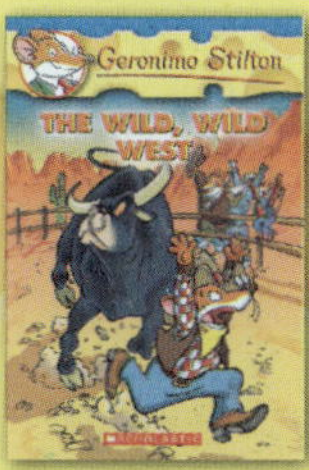


#21 The Wild, Wild West

#22 The Secret of Cacklefur Castle

A Christmas Tale

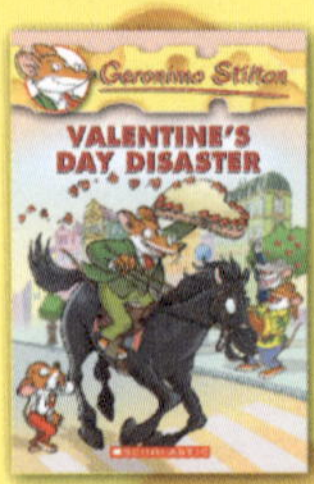

#23 Valentine's Day Disaster

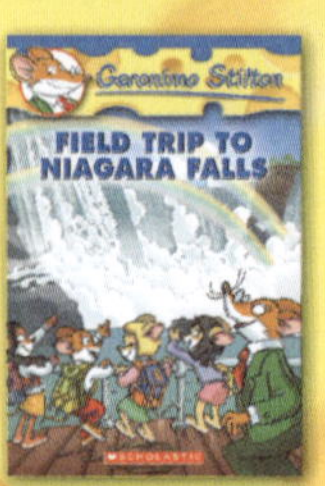

#24 Field Trip to Niagara Falls

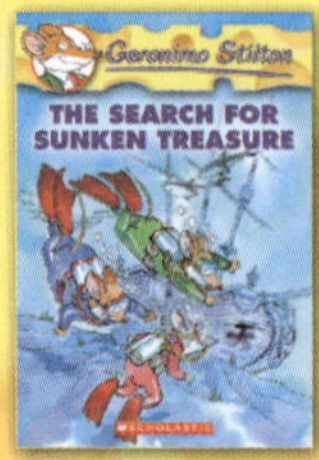

#25 The Search for Sunken Treasure

#26 The Mummy with No Name

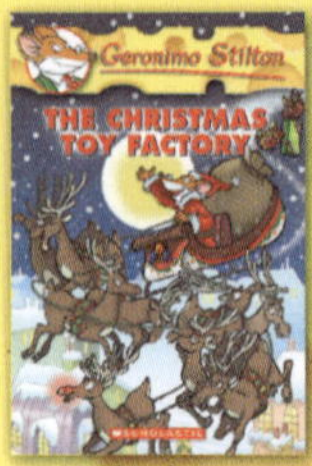

#27 The Christmas Toy Factory

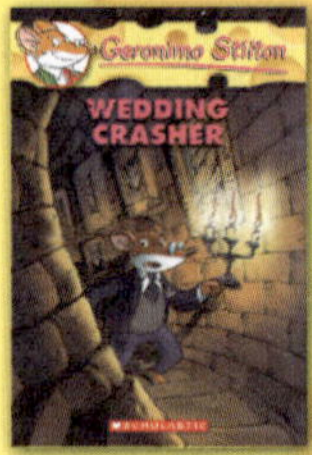

#28 Wedding Crasher

#29 Down and Out Down Under

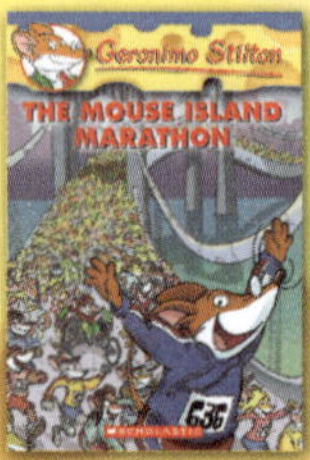

#30 The Mouse Island Marathon

#31 The Mysterious Cheese Thief

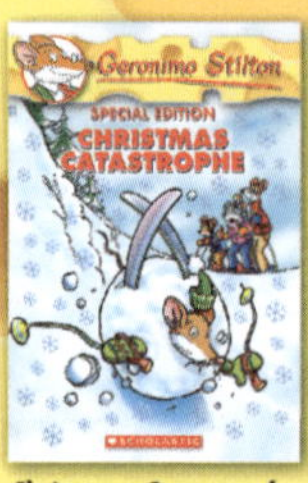

Christmas Catastrophe

#32 Valley of the Giant Skeletons

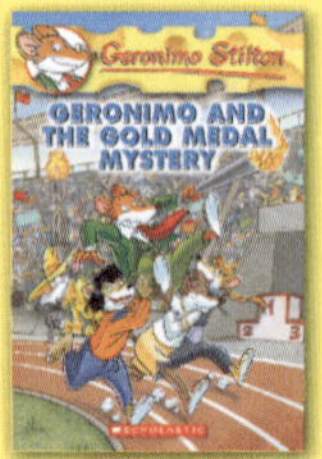

#33 Geronimo and the Gold Medal Mystery

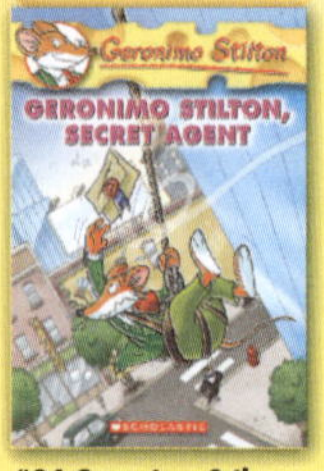

#34 Geronimo Stilton, Secret Agent

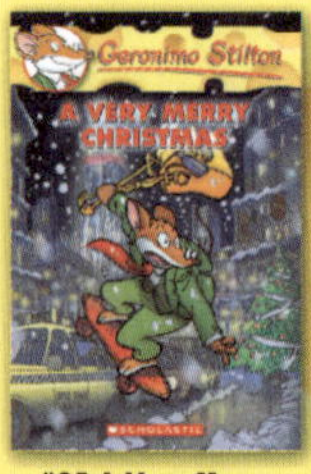

#35 A Very Merry Christmas

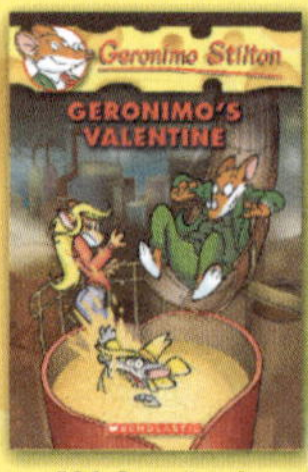

#36 Geronimo's Valentine

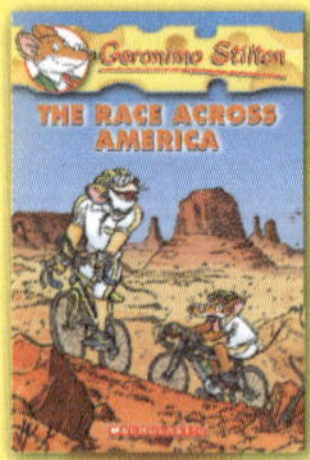

#37 The Race Across America

#38 A Fabumouse School Adventure

#39 Singing Sensation

#40 The Karate Mouse

#41 Mighty Mount Kilimanjaro

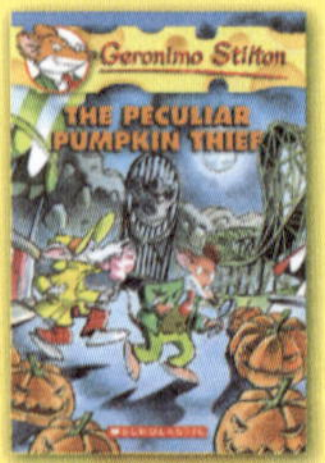

#42 The Peculiar Pumpkin Thief

#43 I'm Not a Supermouse!

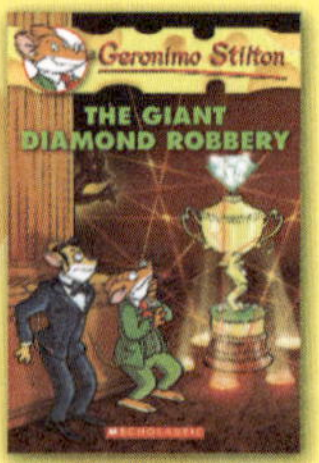

#44 The Giant Diamond Robbery

#45 Save the White Whale!

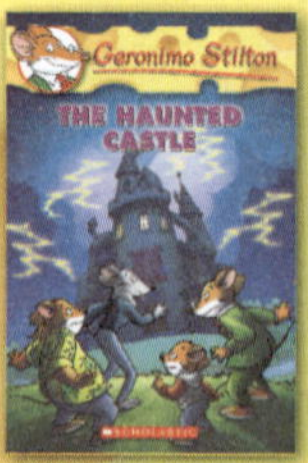

#46 The Haunted Castle

#47 Run for the Hills, Geronimo!

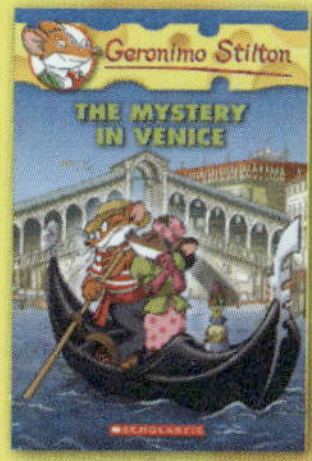


#48 The Mystery in Venice

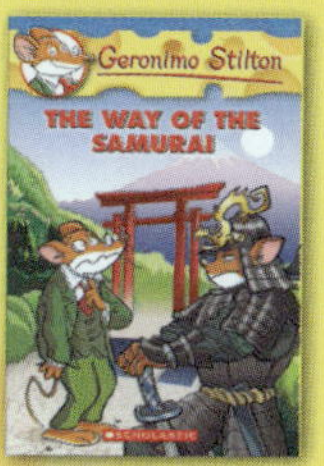


#49 The Way of the Samurai

#50 This Hotel Is Haunted!

#51 The Enormouse Pearl Heist

#52 Mouse in Space!

#53 Rumble in the Jungle

#54 Get into Gear, Stilton!

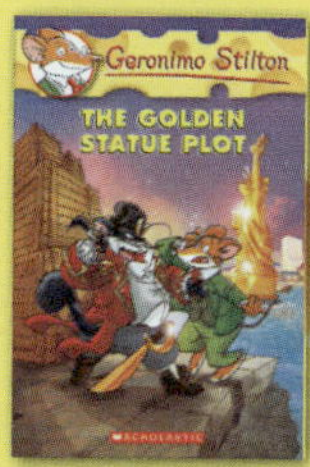


#55 The Golden Statue Plot

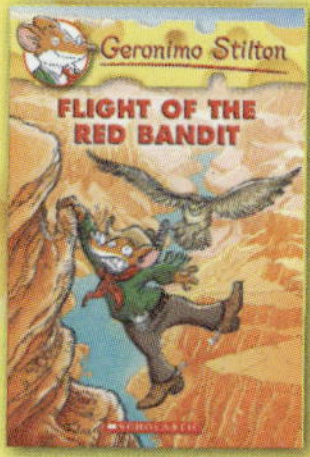


#56 Flight of the Red Bandit

The Hunt for the Golden Book

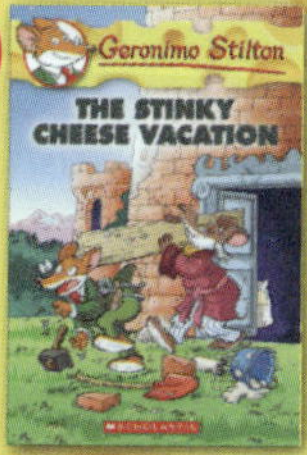


#57 The Stinky Cheese Vacation

#58 The Super Chef Contest

#59 Welcome to Moldy Manor

The Hunt for the Curious Cheese

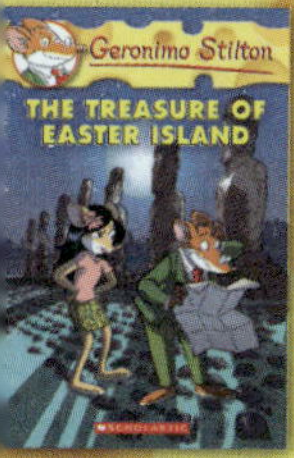


#60 The Treasure of Easter Island

#61 Mouse House Hunter

#62 Mouse Overboard!

The Hunt for the Secret Papyrus

#63 The Cheese Experiment

#64 Magical Mission

#65 Bollywood Burglary

The Hunt for the Hundredth Key

#66 Operation: Secret Recipe

# DON'T MISS ANY HEROMICE BOOKS!

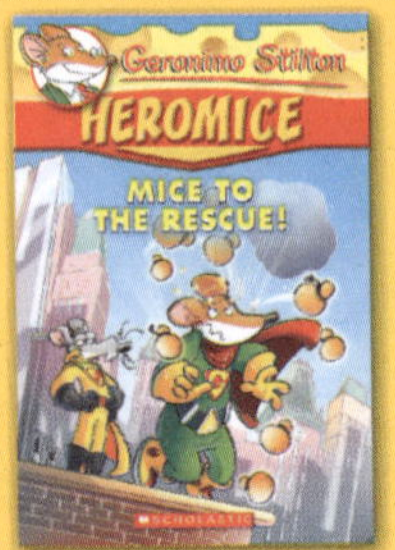


#1 Mice to the Rescue!

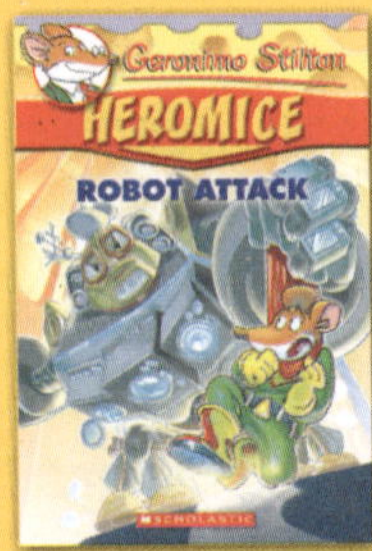


#2 Robot Attack

#3 Flood Mission

#4 The Perilous Plants

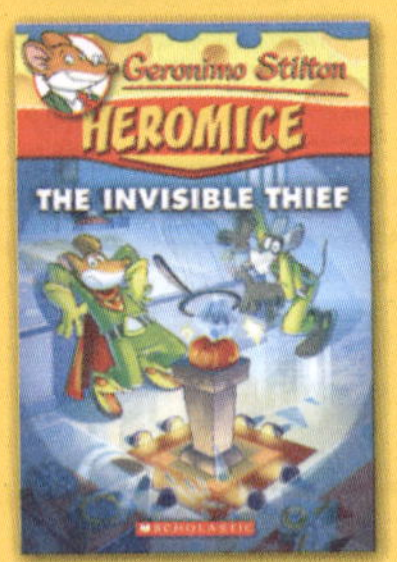


#5 The Invisible Thief

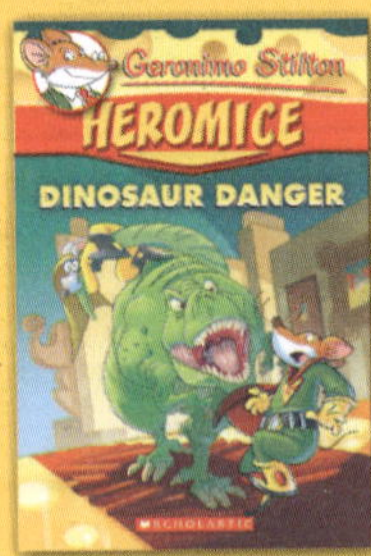


#6 Dinosaur Danger

#7 Time Machine Trouble

#8 Charge of the Clones

# MEET GERONIMO STILTONIX

**He is a spacemouse — the Geronimo Stilton of a parallel universe! He is captain of the spaceship *MouseStar 1*. While flying through the cosmos, he visits distant planets and meets crazy aliens. His adventures are out of this world!**

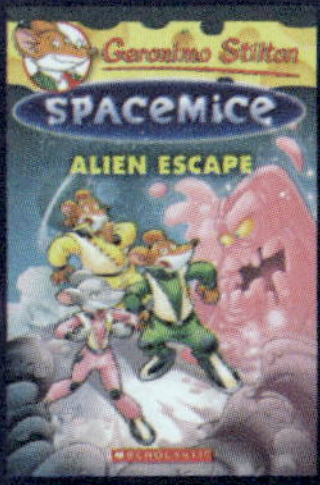


#1 Alien Escape

#2 You're Mine, Captain!

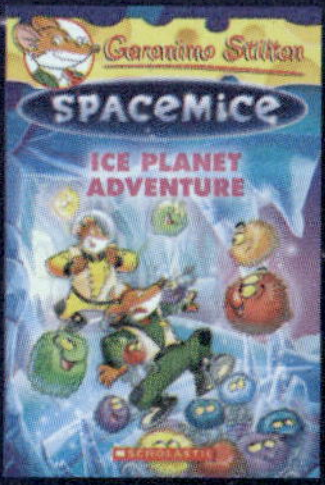


#3 Ice Planet Adventure

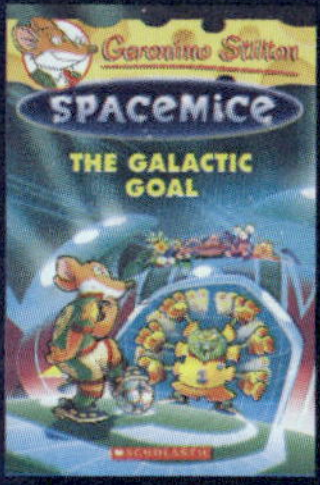


#4 The Galactic Goal

#5 Rescue Rebellion

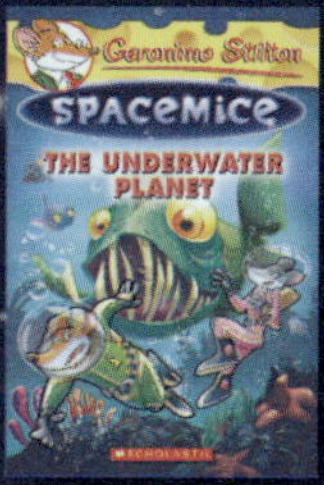


#6 The Underwater Planet

#7 Beware! Space Junk!

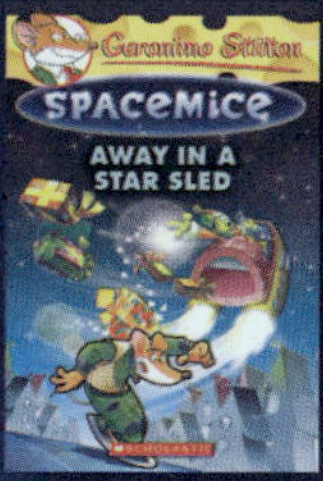


#8 Away in a Star Sled

#9 Slurp Monster Showdown

DEAR MOUSE FRIENDS,
THANKS FOR READING, AND
FAREWELL TILL THE NEXT BOOK.
IT'LL BE ANOTHER
WHISKER-LICKING-GOOD
ADVENTURE, AND THAT'S
A PROMISE!